Rambli

caffein.

Gemma Pybus

BookLeaf
Publishing

Ramblings of the caffeine reliant. © 2022
Gemma Pybus

All rights reserved.

Gemma Pybus asserts the moral right to be
identified as author of this work.

Presentation by *BookLeaf Publishing*

Web: www.bookleafpub.com

E-mail: info@bookleafpub.com

ISBN: 9789357612692

First edition 2022

DEDICATION

To Dean, who always supports this kind of insanity, and to James, Lily and Molly. I love you all very much.

End of an era.

A somber sky,
The silent street,
A knowing nod to those you meet.
Thin black veils and
Hand-tied flowers.
A lone bell tolling every hour.
Stifled cries -
Lonely tears -
The unchanging constant through all these years
Has gone.

Red chair

That moment
When you are reading in your red chair.
Eyes struggling in the dim light
When the sun breaks through the clouds
Illuminating the dust in the air
and making your soul soar.

Wasps

There is nothing lovelier than a wasp.
With a sugary morsel in her grasp.
Her yellow and black sweater, so on-trend,
Nonchalant as you defend
Your lunch.

James

My beautiful boy.
Funny and awkward,
Quiet yet so loud,
With every moment you make me proud.

Your Lego creations, your dinosaur tales,
Your sighs of frustration if things ever fail.
But look at you now: a climber, shark diver,
Head first down a death slide for a crisp new
fiver.

How you have grown, my wonderful son,
I thank the stars every day that I am your mum.

Lily

Peace Lily, Water Lily,
Cat drawing expert Lily
Wild Lily, fire Lily,
Fiercely loyal and loving lily.
Little leopard Lily,
My most beloved flower.

Molly-May

Mol, Molly, mollusc, moomin princess.
Mongoose, Molly-May, our tiny little songstress.
With a doll in your arms and a smile on your
face,
You're the most fabulous Molly in all time and
space.

28th July 2020

Running in the park
My little barefoot hippies.
Ahoy there, shipmate!

29th July 2020

Pulling up the weeds.
Avoiding kids with mower.
I want a combine.

30th July 2020

Banking with children
Stay behind the line with me
Licking the door knobs.

Christmas Haiku

Sparkly Christmastide.
A large, twinkling tree sings
Thanks to the mulled wine.

Slime - how do I hate thee?

Eurgh, my slimy slime. You inspire me to write.
I hate the way you exist, seep and gloop.
Invading the holes in the dining table
Oozing into the carpet.

Let me compare you to a chocolate teapot.
You are more pointless and synthetic.
I look at you upon toy shop shelves
And can think of little more pathetic.

How do I hate you? Let me count the ways.
I hate your nonsensical existence.
But more I hate the fact that you cost three
pounds.
For a bucket of purposeless subsistence.

Now I must away with my angered heart.
Remember my anti-slime words when we're
apart.

A love poem for the awkward

Roses are red,
Violets are blue
I like your trousers
I hope you like mine too.

Orchids are white
Ghost ones are rare
Chickens are fluffy,
And so is your hair.

Daisies are pretty
Daffodils have style
Your headlights are dazzling
And so is your smile.

A sea full of jellyfish

Tedious capture.
A little, brisk jellyfish.
Ribbons in the air.

Evening on deck

Chilly eventide
A golden, thoughtful sun drops
Watching the new moon.

Romantic Ramblings

In the shadows of East Scotland,
A battlefield there lies.
Deserted, the area stands alone
No one can hear its cries.

On a cold winters evening
The land, so cold and bare.
a ghostly figure walks the night,
shadow of a maiden fair.

Her love she lost long, long ago
Yet still, she mourns him sadly.
Walking the night to find him still,
Dedicated to him madly.

She stumbles and falls along the way
On the land, so cold and bare.
She rests now too; shc'll find him soon,
Death of a maiden fair.

Not far away a light appears
A figure greets his wife,
To carry her home once again.
For him she gave her life.

Now a figure walks the moor,
Filled – his heart – with sadness
The one he left so long ago
Enveloped by the blackness.

He searches the moors for answers,
Why did he lose his maid?
Wanders he too, across the earth
And his life begins to fade.

The shadows of forgotten lives
Lie upon the misty moor
The ghostly figure lies to sleep
Never to wake once more

The maiden fair, the hero strong,
Both lie beneath the mist
Along with forgotten memories
The moor the sun long hath kissed.

The souls of many soar above the moor,
Generations lie beneath
But the newcomers – hero and maid
Shall finally together be.

A silent place of beauty here,
Where nature lies alone
You can still hear the faithful too.
Sweet voices amidst an eerie drone.

In the shadows of East Scotland,
A battlefield there lies.
Deserted, the area stands alone
Brings tears to faithful eyes.

Haiku by Drunk AI #1

Frigid eventide
A nosed, gorgeous dolphin skips
enjoying Strictly.

Haiku by Drunk AI #2

Early freezing leap
A red, heavy squirrel stands
before the biscuits.

Haiku by Drunk AI #3

Smoggy London Town
A passionate weasel hunts
Near Madame Tussauds.

Haiku by Drunk AI #4

December Evening
Mr Blobby cries alone.
betrayed by the knife

Haiku by Drunk AI #5

Sainsbury's Car Park
Rollerblading rat children
Stunts by the trollies.

Milton Keynes UK
Ingram Content Group UK Ltd.
UKHW020832280723
425958UK00016B/571

9 789357 612692